A Guide to
HAPPY FAMILY
Cooking

A Guide to
HAPPY FAMILY
Cooking

(Learning to Let Kids Get In Your Way!)

TAMMERIE SPIRES

Good Books

Intercourse, PA 17534
800/762-7171

Design by Dawn J. Ranck
Cover illustration by Cheryl Benner

A GUIDE TO HAPPY FAMILY COOKING
Copyright © 2000 by Good Books, Intercourse, PA 17534
International Standard Book Number: 1-56148-304-4
Library of Congress Catalog Card Number: 00-027913

Library of Congress Cataloging-in-Publication Data

Spires, Tammerie.
    A guide to happy family cooking : letting kids get in your
way! / Tammerie Spires.
        p.cm.
    Includes bibliographical references and index.
    ISBN 1-5614-304-4
    1. Cookery. I. Title
TX714.X643 2000
641.5--dc21   00-027913

Dedication

To my mother,
for turning me loose in the kitchen
at a very early age

Acknowledgments

I am blessed to be bookended by my parents—who have enthusiastically eaten my cooking for 25 years—and by my children—who are talented and enthusiastic little cooks, and who have put up with me while I learned to get out of the way in the kitchen.

Thanks to good neighbor and beloved friend Annette Albrecht for recipe-testing and, more importantly, for proof-reading; of course, any remaining errors in the text have to be laid at my feet! And thanks to Annette and Wayne's daughter, Jenny, for many hours of cook-talk and more than a little recipe review.

Thank you to all the families who shared and tested recipes and ideas, especially Julianna Borsodi Araya and her kids, Daniel and Esther Araya; Janee Duval and her niece, Laurie; Barbara Graber and daughters, Katherine and Kristin; Sandra Kelley and her kids, Bridgette and Jackson; Ellen Raff and her son, Christopher.

Thanks to my favorite sisters(-in-law), Rebecca Spires and Crystal Spires. Bec helped me decipher the Pink Soup recipe after we delighted in something similar at Café Pasqual in Santa Fe, NM; Crystal and her kids, Austin and Julie, test-drove lots of recipes.

Thanks also go to my other mother, Nancy Schmitz, the best mother-in-law a woman could ask for and the source of the recipe for Nan's Gazpacho.

And thank *you* for picking up this book. I hope it brings you many happy hours in the most popular room of the house—the kitchen.

— Tammerie Spires

Table of Contents

1.

ONE WAY TO A CHILD'S HEART . . .

. . . is through the kitchen! Have you noticed the fastest way to gather your child/ren around you? Just start rattling pots and pans in the kitchen or getting out the mixing bowls, and any mobile kid will usually come running (or crawling). "Whatcha makin', Mom?" the older ones ask, as the younger ones grab a leg and pull up to the counter.

Then there's the day when—usually pretty soon after a child learns to talk—your child asks to help you do whatever it is you're doing.

Now if you're like me, your first inclination might be to say, "Well, honey, I know you want to help, but this knife is sharp." Or, "Maybe next time, sweetie. Mommy (or Daddy, as the case may be) is in a little bit of a hurry right now." Or, "This is kind of complicated . . . ."

Those are all perfectly reasonable things to say to a child. But sooner or later you may get the feeling that you are missing an opportunity. You could be. I know *I* was, and—though I'm embarrassed to admit it—here's why.

I may not be the best cook, but I am quite probably one of the most perfectionist of cooks. I want to do things *my* way. As a result, I don't tolerate helpers well, large or small, because they don't necessarily do things my way.

I'd like to say I had an epiphany that helped me let go of my perfectionist attitudes and become more accepting of having my kids cook with me, but I haven't. What I do have is a growing awareness that my selfishness in this area is cheating my kids and me out of a lot of fun and useful learning. So, I'm working to get over my attitude. Here's why I'm trying, and here's what's helping me.

Why Cook with Kids?

There are a world of reasons, but this is meant to be a concise book, so I'll just give you my top three:

It's quality time with your kids. Have you ever noticed when your kids talk to you? Usually when you are involved in doing something else: driving somewhere, washing dishes, clearing the yard. Cooking gives you one more activity to do together, and you can *eat* the results.

Kids learn so many by-product lessons: shapes, sizes, measuring, new tastes, different uses of foodstuffs, volumes, behavior of liquids, chemical and physical changes in foodstuffs, autonomy, how to clean things . . . I could go on and on.

The more boys that learn to cook, the more men there will someday be that know how to cook. Teach that boy to cook (and clean up after himself). Your son's friends—and possibly his future spouse—will nominate you for sainthood. This is not meant to be a sexist comment; obviously, it's good for girls *and* boys to learn to cook. It's just that too many men don't cook because they didn't grow up doing it. Nuff said.

What's Helping Me Cook with My Kids

I've finally become clear about what my boundaries are in the kitchen. When I'm in a hurry to get a meal on the table, or when I'm cooking something that is special to me, I politely and firmly decline offers of assistance that are not actually helpful or welcome.

On the other hand, I *do* now set aside times with my kids when we make things they like to make, or that they want to learn to make, or that they like to eat. And I have found that, given enough time, blessed with the right temperament, and stocked with appropriate skills, ingredients and recipes, kids *can* be a joy in the kitchen, and sometimes even a help!

What do time and temperament have to do with cooking, you may ask? Well,when it comes to cooking with kids . . .

It's about Time . . . and Temperament!

If you're like me, cooking is one of your favorite creative outlets, and you've decided you want to share this love with your kids. But maybe, like me, your first few attempts did not go so well. Maybe the mess was annoying, the little hands couldn't quite manage, or you found yourself using *that* tone of voice as you testily finished the job.

Or, maybe cooking is not your favorite thing to do, and you'd really like your kids to grow up feeling more comfortable and/or happy in the kitchen than you do.

Here's the most important lesson I've learned.

> ## *Happy Cook Principle 1:*
>
> **Make time—and *take* time—for cooking with kids.**

I think the first and most important ingredient in any recipe is *time*: time to show kids how to do the task, time to let kids do it themselves, time to let them do it wrong, time to try again if necessary. This is especially important when you are teaching your child/ren new skills.

Conversely, when time is in short supply—for instance, when I am in a hurry to get dinner on the table—well, that's not a great time to teach a child new skills. But it is a great time for a child to take care of a task that he or she is already familiar with, and that he or she can complete with little supervision.

Unless, of course, evenings are not a good time for your child/ren. This has to do with a child's *temperament*, and that's another thing to keep in mind:

Happy Cook Principle 2:

When cooking with kids, *temperament* **is as important as temperature.**

You wouldn't ignore a recipe's instructions as to when and how hot to preheat the oven. Well, knowing your child/ren's temperament and working to its advantage is as important as minding the oven's temperature.

How does your child like to play and learn? Does she love to talk about what you're going to do first, or does she like to dive right in? Does he like to watch you do it a while, and then decide whether to try it himself? Is she picky about getting her hands dirty, or does she love hands-on messes? Does he want to have his own little project alongside yours, or will nothing do but to have his hands all over what *you're* doing?

What time of day is best for your child? Is she a morning person, or does she come alive at five? Is he cranky right after a nap, or is that a well-rested time to try new things?

Is it hard for her to transition from one activity to another? Or is he always in a rush to get on to the next thing?

Take into consideration your knowledge about your child/ren's work and play habits. Accommodate your kitchen activities accordingly, and cooking with kids will go more smoothly.

Okay, But Cooking What?

Let me tell you about the rest of this book. Coming right up, you'll find a **Recipes** section with a manageable number of instructive and delicious dishes to try with your child/ren. You can try the recipes in any order, whenever you like. If you do work through them in the order provided, they will help you teach your child/ren in a way that builds and refines skills over time. You may want to set aside a certain time with your child/ren each week to try a recipe or two, with the purpose of learning the skills that each recipe teaches.

Mixed throughout the recipes are brief sidebars subtitled "What's the Occasion?" These will suggest ways you and your kids can use these recipes to celebrate or create special times together with family and friends.

Any excuse to get together with friends or family and share good food will do, but some excuses demand more than others. Don't you love it when someone makes a fuss for you? Admit it, you do! And so do your kids. They will also love getting to create a fuss for themselves, their friends and family. "What's the Occasion?" sidebars cover many of the celebration-inspiring occasions and seasons around which you and your kids might want to create a fuss. The recipes in this book will help you pull it off with panache!

Another way to use this section is to pick an occasion and spend a few weeks helping your kids gain the skills they need to accomplish the dishes for its menu. Then let them use what they've learned for the desired occasion or seasonal activity.

The last section, **Resources**, points you to magazines, websites, and other sources of information that can contribute to the fun of cooking with your kids. You'll also find, scattered throughout the book, a series of **Happy Cook Principles.** These are general concepts that I believe help keep the "happy" in happy family cooking.

Consider the Following . . .

I have written this book to guide an adult who is, in turn, guiding a child. Directions in the recipes suggest which activities adults should do or help with, such as turning on the oven or cutting that requires a sharp knife. All the rest of the activities are ones that a child should be able to complete with some instruction and supervision from an adult. (Of course, whether you allow the time for your child to roll out one Flaky Pizza [see page 89]—or all 20!—is up to you.)

With this in mind, please note that I will not preface every direction in the recipes with "Show your child how to . . ." or "Ask your child to . . .". Rather, I will assume that you (the adult involved) are reading the instructions, and then talking with and working with your child to complete the needed tasks. You are aware of what your child is capable of and interested in doing.

A note on safety. Most recipes use the simple utensils found in a place setting: a safe knife, spoon, and fork. (Please read "Safe Cutting, Safe Cook" on pages 20-22.) Many of the recipes can be made without heat from an oven or stove. But there *are* recipes that require use of a sharp utensil, such as a knife or can opener, and that require the use of heat to cook the food. That brings me to:

Happy Cook Principle 3:

Teach kids *how* to take care in the kitchen.

Do your cooking child/ren a favor. Before beginning the recipes in this book, teach them how to handle knives safely (see pages 20-22), as well as hot cooking areas like the stove and oven (see pages 30-31). I can't predict your child's ages, skill levels, or the degree to which they will mind your instructions. You have to decide on safety rules in advance, and be sure they are clear. I would recommend practice of a "stop" drill. Teach your child how to stop immediately and safely whatever he or she is doing when you call "stop!" This will help you help your child stop short of danger.

Children who are old enough to read and interpret recipes can certainly use this book alone, but the recipes are written assuming an adult is involved. Please be aware of the sharp utensils and hot cooking techniques required in some of the recipes, and be sure your older child has either the skills or the supervision needed to be safe.

But don't let recipe references to "an" adult or "a" child limit you to consider cooking as a one adult/one child activity. Many of these recipes can involve several children or adults at a time. The more, the merrier!

Finally, if you are not familiar with the ingredients or techniques used in a recipe, by all means try it yourself before involving your child/ren. By doing that, you'll know better where they might need help, and they won't get frustrated waiting for you to figure out something.

2.

THE RECIPES

You and I both know there's a world of recipes out there that work for cooking with kids. Well, I whittled that immense list down to the 30-odd recipes that follow, because these recipes will help you help your child/ren learn basic cooking skills. As they refine those skills, they will be able to complete these recipes more independently (though of course small children must always be supervised in the kitchen).

Each recipe mentions what skills are being taught within it. I also suggest ways in which many of these recipes can be edited creatively by substituting or adding different ingredients.

Within each section (Appetizers, Soups, Salads, Entrees, and Desserts), the recipes build in degrees of skills required or number of cooking techniques used. However, all the recipes are ones that can be completed by children fairly independently, once a child has learned all the skills.

THE RECIPES

Many of the recipes use ingredients or result in dishes your child/ren may be unfamiliar with. Try them anyway! Sometimes the best way to get a child to try a new food is for that child to have had a hand in preparing it. And the second best way may be for your child to get rave reviews on that special dish from others!

A note on ingredients and appliances. I have selected mostly recipes your child/ren can prepare without great reliance on convenience foods or fancy tools. Most recipes use the simple utensils that are found in a place setting. But in a few cases, I do suggest the use of convenience foods, primarily to let the kids get cooking sooner rather than later. And you will see mention of a food processor in one recipe to save you from endless chopping—but endless chopping is provided as an alternative!

APPETIZERS

How many times have you snacked your way through some great appetizers, sat down to dinner, and realized you were not really hungry? The fact is, nobody doesn't like appetizers! And the ones presented here are good enough and easy enough to make a light meal.

The recipes in this chapter can be thought of as belonging to two families. The Black Bean Dip and Guacamole go great with the Homemade "Chips," and either works as an appetizer for any American or Southwestern menu. The Tomato and Tapenade Toppings go great with the Bruschetta (garlic toasts) and make lovely starters for any American or Italian menu. But each recipe stands alone quite nicely, too.

You'll notice the use of dried spices in many of these recipes. I heartily recommend using fresh herbs and spices wherever available and whenever possible (which will be more often if you plant an herb garden; see Resources, pages 115-116). My kids are certainly accustomed to going out into the herb garden by our side door and snipping some oregano, rosemary, or basil. But I also realize that not every family has an herb garden located so conveniently, so I'm not going to be snooty about herbs. It's more important to get going and to have fun.

That said, you will see some recipes where I definitely recommend fresh herbs because their contribution is critical: for instance, the fresh basil recommended in the Tomato Topper dish. But for many cases, dried spices work fine, have a longer shelf life, and are easier for beginning cooks to measure and use. All right, let's get cooking!

In sight, in mind . . .

I read voraciously as a pregnant person and as a new parent . . . until my firstborn began to be awake much of the day and too often at night.

One of the best pieces of advice I remember getting from one of those early parenting books was to stock a floor-level kitchen cabinet with wooden spoons, old pots, and unbreakable bowls. Furthermore, we were to leave that cabinet without a child-proofing device so the kids could get into it whenever they wanted. That helped keep the little ones busy while I was busy, and let us stay together in the kitchen without them getting underfoot.

And I'm pretty sure that cabinet and its treasures are responsible for the way Harper wields a whisk today!

Black Bean Dip

Skills taught: rinsing, draining, smashing, measuring, cutting, and mixing.

Ingredients:
  10-12 cherry tomatoes
  2 cans black beans (15-oz. each)
  1 Tbsp. dried, minced onions
  1 tsp. powdered garlic
  1 tsp. powdered cumin
  Salt and pepper to taste

1. Remove any stems or leaves from the tomatoes, and then rinse the tomatoes in a colander. Take the tomatoes out and put them on a towel to dry.

Note: An adult should open the cans of black beans so that the child does not have to use a sharp can opener or risk injury on the sharp edge of the can. Show your child how to avoid the can edges when using a spoon to scoop the beans into the colander or strainer.

2. If you want a thicker dip, or are concerned about excess salt in canned foods, rinse the beans, too. Give your child a small measuring cup or big spoon to scoop beans onto a dinner plate. Show your child how to smash the beans against the plate to make a rough paste. Scrape the paste into a bowl (choose one big enough to hold all your ingredients), and scoop some

more beans onto the plate. Continue smashing portions of beans until they are all smashed and in the bowl.

3. Measure and add the dried ingredients. Add a pinch of salt and pepper (you can add more to taste later, if necessary).

Note! Please read "Safe Cutting, Safe Cook" (pages 20-22) for information on finding and using a child-safe knife.

4. Show your child how to use a safe knife to quarter the tomatoes. First, cut the tomatoes in half, and then cut the halves in half. (You may need to cut the tomatoes into more pieces than quarters; you want to produce bean-sized pieces. But bigger chunks are okay if that's what your child can accomplish.) Scrape chopped tomatoes into the bowl.

Hint: Laurie, age 7, helped test this recipe. She liked using a plastic knife best. These have about the right amount of serration and are small and light, which is good for kids. As to the recipe's outcome? Laurie said, "It was goo-oo-ood!" Her Aunt Janee said the potato masher worked better for them than a fork and plate for smashing beans.

---

5. Stir all ingredients together until well combined (i.e., you can't distinguish any one ingredient very well). Serve with any kind of chip (note the recipe for Homemade "Chips" on page 27). This dip can be eaten right away, but it will taste better if you let it sit for 30

minutes at room temperature. It can be made the day before and refrigerated. You can serve it right out of the fridge, or let it come to room temperature.

Variations:

- *This dip can be made with pinto beans, too.*
- *For a pretty dip, garnish with a dollop of sour cream, stirred in a bit so it leaves a white swirl in the dip, and an oregano sprig.*
- *For a really quick dip, mix smashed beans with your favorite bottled salsa (keeping in mind your child/ren's or guests' heat tolerance), and skip the chopping and addition of dried ingredients.*
- *For a smoother dip, put all ingredients in a food processor, whirl it up, and pour it out.*
- *For great presentation, make two dips—one with black beans and one with pinto beans—and pour them into the same bowl side by side, but don't mix them together. The slight color contrast is really pretty.*

Safe Cutting, Safe Cook

It's very important to teach your child safe knife techniques before he or she uses a knife of any kind. This involves selecting a safe knife and teaching and practicing safe cutting techniques.

The Safe Knife

The first task is to select a knife that works for your child. You can work with what's already in your kitchen, or shop for something in particular. In recipes, I will refer to this as your child/ren's "safe knife."

At our house, our everyday tableware includes a knife in the place setting which has a lightly serrated edge on the outer half of the knife blade. My kids use this for a safe knife because the size is manageable, the blade is sharp enough but not too sharp, and several of these knives are always available.

Other options? On the one hand, one of my testers was happy for her child to use her Pampered Chef "child-safe knife." On the other hand, another tester found that best tool was a small plastic knife of the type you get at fast-food restaurants.

Use out-of-the-drawer thinking, and you may come up with ideas like these: a rolling pizza cutter (these are usually very sharp; make sure it has a finger guard and supervise closely), children's plastic scissors (they go right in the dishwasher), a rolling pasta cutter (these tend not to be so sharp), or press-down metal or plastic cookie or biscuit cutters.

You may want to experiment with what you have to decide what's best for you.

Cutting Techniques

A good way to begin cutting is with something small and soft that will cut easily and not roll around. Commercial or homemade play-dough is fun to cut and can be formed into different shapes to practice different kinds of cutting. Soft-cooked vegetables such as potatoes or carrots also present good shapes and textures for cutting practice.

Once you've selected a safe knife, tell your child/ren that this is the knife to use always, until you tell him or her otherwise. Show your child/ren how to:

- Keep the hand holding the item to be cut a safe distance back from the knife.

- Curl the tips of the fingers (on the holding hand) under, away from the knife, and press them into the food being cut.

- Grip the knife so that the hand is on the handle, with the thumb and forefinger pinching the blade right in front of the handle and the other fingers curling around and under the handle.

- Cut slowly, with back-and-forth sawing motions.

- Move the cut piece away before cutting another.

- Put the knife away safely before moving on to other activities.

Assess the child's dexterity and ability with the safe knife before moving on to any other kind of cutting activity or tool.

And remember: Be sure your child knows to never, ever use a knife without an adult supervising.

Guacamole

Skills taught/practiced: rinsing, cutting, scraping, smashing, reaming, chopping, and mixing.

Ingredients:
10-12 cherry tomatoes
1 lemon *or* lime
4-6 avocados (store in paper sack to ripen;
    do not put in fridge)
1 Tbsp. dried, minced onions
1 tsp. powdered garlic
1 tsp. powdered cumin
Salt and pepper to taste

1. Remove any stems or leaves from the tomatoes, and rinse the tomatoes in a colander. Take the tomatoes out and put them on a towel to dry.

2. Give your child a safe knife to cut the lemon or lime in half. Show your child how to scrape out the seeds with the tip of the knife and how to use a reamer to juice the lemon or lime over the bowl. Pick out any errant seeds. Lemon or lime juice will keep the avocado from browning, so pour the juice into the bowl before adding the avocados.

3. *Note*: An adult should cut open each avocado by ringing the rind stem to stern and back around with a sharp knife, cutting through to the pit at the core.

Twist the two halves apart, exposing the pit. Test the

pit. If it feels loose in the avocado's flesh, dig it out with a spoon. Simply scrape any avocado flesh clinging to the removed pit into the bowl. (Pick a bowl big enough to hold all your ingredients and still have room for stirring.)

Hint: What to do with the pit? I never liked putting it in the guacamole; it's more fun to plant it! Yes, there's a project for the occasional gardener . . .

If the pit is tightly embedded in the avocado flesh, an adult can use this simple technique to remove it (simple, but too dangerous for kids; ask them to stand back a bit). Lay the avocado on your cutting board and whack into the pit with a sharp knife. That should embed the knife in the pit. Give it a twist and the pit should pop out. (If it doesn't, your avocados are not ripe. Put the rest of them back in the paper sack and let them ripen another day or two.)

4. Show your child how to cup the avocado half in his/her palm, and make slits in the avocado flesh with a safe knife, like stripes running from top to bottom. Do not try to cut through the rind; use the rind as a bowl to work in. Then, turn the avocado a quarter turn and make slits running the other way. Now use a spoon to scoop the resulting avocado cubes out onto a plate, and smash the avocado cubes with a fork into a rough pulp or paste. Scrape the paste into the bowl and stir it into the lemon or lime juice.

5. When all the avocado is in the bowl and mixed

with lemon juice, show your child how to measure and add the powdered spices. Add a pinch of salt and pepper; you can add more later to taste, if necessary. Stir in the powdered ingredients.

6. Using a safe knife, show your child how to quarter the tomatoes. First, cut the tomatoes in half, and then cut the halves in half. (You may need to cut the tomatoes into more pieces than quarters; you want to produce bean-sized pieces. But bigger chunks are okay if that's what your child can accomplish.) Help your child scrape chopped tomatoes into the bowl, and mix them in.

Variations:

- *For a pretty dip, garnish the top with a few thin slices of tomato and/or lemon.*
- *For a really quick dip, mix smashed guacamole with your favorite bottled salsa, and skip the chopping and dried ingredients. But don't use a food processor; guacamole is supposed to be chunky.*

St. Patrick's Day Party

What's a St. Patrick's Day party without Green Noodles? (See page 98.) I know, Green Noodles is really an Italian dish (pesto-sauced pasta), and St. Patrick's has an Irish feel to it, but Green Noodles are just so . . . green! How can you resist?

You could use Guacamole (page 23) as an appetizer, and accompany the main dish with Cucumber Moons, found on page 45 (yes, these are some strange flavor combinations, but they are so-o-o nice and green).

You could even make a bread with a swirl of green food coloring.

Lemon-lime-flavored ginger ale or club soda with lime slices makes a festive beverage. And just about every grocery or home-decorating store will have St. Patrick's Day decorations and tableware, if you like.

For dessert, a Fruit Salad that goes heavy on kiwis and honeydew melons will have the right hue—and a great taste!

Homemade "Chips"

Skills taught/practiced: cutting, seasoning, baking.

Ingredients:
1 package wonton wrappers,
  or 12 corn tortillas,
  or 4 6-inch pita bread rounds
1 can butter-flavored *or* olive oil cooking spray
Salt, pepper and other seasonings
  (see Variations)

For Wonton Chips:

1. **Note**: An adult should turn on the oven and close-ly supervise its use (see pages 30-31).
Preheat oven (conventional or toaster oven) to 375°F.

2. Cut each wonton wrapper in half diagonally with a lightly serrated butter or table setting knife and lay on a cookie sheet. You should be able to cut several at a time, since they are thin.

3. Spray the wonton wrapper chips with water and bake 8-10 minutes, or until lightly browned and crispy. Watch closely to see that they don't burn.

For Corn Tortilla Chips

1. **Note**: An adult should turn on the oven and closely supervise its use (see pages 30-31).
Preheat oven (conventional or toast oven) to 375°F.

2. Cut each tortilla with a safe knife into quarter

wedges.(Show your child how to cut in half, and then in half again.)

3. Spread the wedges on an ungreased cookie sheet, coat with cooking spray, and lightly salt and pepper.

4. Bake the tortilla chips for 10-15 minutes, or until lightly browned and crispy. Watch closely to see that they don't burn.

Hint: Christopher, age 4, helped test this recipe. His favorite part was cutting up the tortillas because he got to use the kitchen shears. He also liked doing the vegetable spray and shaking on spices. Christopher's mom, Ellen, says, "I like the recipe because I'm addicted to tortilla chips. But if I make these periodically, I will get less salt and less hydrogenated fat than if I eat the commercial variety. So I'm a big fan of this recipe!"

For Pita Chips

1. *Note:* An adult should turn on the oven and closely supervise its use (see pages 30-31).

Preheat oven (conventional or toaster oven) to 375°F.

2. Show your child how to cut with a safe knife through the outside edge of the pita to make two circles of pita bread.

3. Separate the circles and cut each into six wedges with a safe knife. (You may want to cut little marks to show your child where to start.)

4. Spread the wedges on an ungreased cookie sheet, coat with cooking spray, and lightly salt and pepper.

5. Bake the pita wedges for 10-15 minutes, or until lightly browned and crispy. Watch closely to see that they don't burn.

Variations:

- *Wonton chips can be made into a sweet treat: after spraying with water, sprinkle with cinnamon-sugar. Bake as above.*
- *After spraying tortilla chips with cooking spray, brush them with a mixture of lime juice and a dash of cumin, garlic powder, and salt and pepper.*
- *You can season the pita wedges with garlic salt, or lemon pepper, or both.*

Safe Oven, Safe Cook

Before using the oven the first time, please go over safe usage practices with your child/ren. Again, you know your child, your utensils, and your oven better than I do. I can't envision every situation, so let me just provide some pointers. Of course, these are similar to the stovetop considerations:

- Teach your child/ren how to turn the oven on and off safely. If you don't want to teach them to turn it on yet, consider teaching them to turn it off. The day may come when you need them to do that, when you have your hands full with something else.

- Teach your child/ren what "hot" means: hold their hands and get close enough to a safe source of heat to feel the "hot." As something cooks, explain that the same thing can happen to us if we get too close to the heat. Explain that a burn accident can happen even if we are being very careful, and that heat and flame are not something to fool around with.

- Teach your child/ren to work "remotely," i.e., using something other than their hands to manipulate foods. This extends to always using hotpads when approaching or picking up a pan or a pot.

- Teach your child/ren to keep a safe distance from the oven when the heat is on, especially when an adult is opening the oven door to check on or remove some food. Escaping steam can scald.

Gauge **very carefully** to see when your child is ready to work around the oven and put things in and take things out. One good practice is to drill with putting cold pans full of water in and out of a cold oven first.

And remember: Be sure your child knows to never, ever use an oven without an adult supervising.

Tomato Topper

Skills taught/practiced: cutting and mixing.

Ingredients:
  3 or 4 ripe tomatoes
  1/4 cup olive oil
  2 or more garlic cloves (to taste)
  10 or more pitted olives (to taste)
  Salt and pepper

1. Remove any stems or leaves from the tomatoes, and rinse the tomatoes in a colander. Put them on a towel to dry.

2. Measure the olive oil into a bowl big enough to hold all ingredients.

3. Separate several cloves from the garlic head.

Note: An adult should cut off the top and bottom edges of each clove. Then a child or an adult can smash the clove. Put the clove under something heavy like a metal spatula, and then bang down on it with your fist. Splat! goes the clove. Now pick the garlic meat out of the papery husk and cut the meat into finer bits with a safe knife. Put into bowl with olive oil.

4. Use a safe knife to cut the olives into little pieces. Mix them into the bowl with the olive oil and the garlic. (Putting these ingredients into the oil first helps flavor the oil.)

5. Use a safe knife to cut up the tomatoes. If using large tomatoes (i.e., larger than cherry tomatoes), an adult may first want to cut the stem area out, or slice off the top if it is fairly flat. Then a child can cut the tomatoes in half and cut the halves in half. (You may need to cut the tomatoes into more pieces than quarters; you want to produce bean-sized pieces. Bigger chunks are okay if that's what your child can accomplish; you can chop them a little finer if necessary.) Scrape chopped tomatoes into the bowl and mix them in.

6. Rinse the basil leaves and tear them into little pieces. Stir them in and add some pepper. (If you did not use olives, you can add a pinch or two of salt.) If your child wants to use the safe knife to cut the basil, that's fine, but tearing works, too.

Variations:
- *You can leave the olives out, or reduce the garlic, but don't leave the garlic out altogether. (I love Kalamata olives, and I use lots! One of my kids loves black olives, and the other kid only likes them sometimes. If your kids like olives, they'll love them in this recipe, and the next.)*
- *The great thing about Tomato Topper is that it's great on Bruschetta (garlic toast; recipe coming up), on angel hair pasta or any other kind of pasta, and on any kind of cooked rice. It even goes well with bite-sized chunks of steamed new potatoes, green beans, and/or zucchini!*

33

Tapenade

Skills taught/practiced: cutting, mixing, using a food processor (if you want!).

Ingredients:
2 1/2 cups drained, pitted olives
   (2 6- or 8-oz cans; see Variations for types)
2-3 garlic cloves
1-2 Tbsp. olive oil
4-oz. jar capers, drained
4-oz. jar pimientos
Pepper

1. Cut *half* the olives into pea-sized pieces and set aside. Put the other half of the olives into the bowl of a food processor or blender.

2. Have an adult cut the ends off the garlic cloves, and then a child or an adult can smash the cloves. Put each clove under something heavy like a metal spatula, and then bang down on it with your fist. Splat! goes the clove.

3. Now pick the garlic meat out of the papery husk and cut the meat into halves or quarters with a safe knife.

4. Put into the bowl of a food processor or blender, along with the olives you already put in there, plus the capers and pimiento (if necessary, cut pimiento pieces to a size that's uniform with the other ingredients).

5. Whirl the ingredients to a chunky paste, and then scrape into a bowl. If you don't want to use a food processor, you can use a mortar and pestle, or simply chop all ingredients very fine. (Please plan ahead to have plenty of time for this.)

6. Mix in the pea-sized olive bits and pepper to taste, and serve.

Note: This spread can be made ahead and refrigerated, but if you're using it as a spread, it'll taste best if you bring it back to room temperature.

Variations:
- *Regular canned black or green olives work fine, but for a special taste use Kalamata or other Mediterranean-style olives. I like to use a mix of green and black olives; I think it tastes better and looks prettier.*
- *A teaspoon of fresh oregano and/or fresh thyme is a nice touch.*
- *If your kids like anchovies (yeah, right!), add 3 or 4 anchovy fillets. A teaspoon of Thai fish sauce can give the same taste.*
- *You can use this as a dip, or on pizza, or on potatoes. Tastes good mixed into pasta or rice, too.*
- *You can spread Tapenade on Bruschetta before toasting. Cover it with grated Parmesan or Romano cheese for a special touch.*

Bruschetta

Skills taught/practiced: cutting, seasoning, baking.

Ingredients:
1 baguette (French bread)
    or 1 ciabatta (slipper-shaped Italian bread)
Olive oil
3-4 garlic cloves
Salt and pepper

1. Use a serrated bread knife to cut the bread into one-inch slices. Please review safe knife handling techniques with your child (see pages 20-22).
2. Pour olive oil into a small bowl. Use a pastry brush to spread it onto the bread.
3. Have an adult cut the ends off the garlic cloves, and then a child or an adult can cut the cloves into halves with a safe knife. Pick the garlic meat out of the papery husks. Rub each garlic clove half firmly over the oiled bread. (You can lightly sprinkle the bread with garlic powder, but it won't taste as good and it's not as much fun. It is faster, though . . . unless your sprinkling turns to dumping! Then you have to start over.)
4. Lightly salt and pepper the bread (unless you are going to put on an olive Tapenade; that is so salty it needs no extra salt, and if it is peppery, the bread needs no pepper, either).

5. Toast in a toaster oven set to light or medium, or grill under the broiler, watching closely, or on the barbecue or gas grill for a Tuscan touch!

6. Serve with additional olive oil for dipping, or with various toppings such as the Tomato Topper (page 32) or Tapenade (page 34).

Variations:

- *You can put the toppings on before toasting.*
- *You can top with grated cheese: pecorino Romano is my favorite, but a nice Parmesan or mozzarella is good, too.*
- *Spread with softened Brie, goat cheese, or cream cheese.*

Turning the Tables on Mom and Dad

(adaptable for Mother's Day, Father's Day, or Any Day!)

Of course, Moms and Dads can pick their favorite recipes, or one of the parents can make suggestions as to what might be nice. If the kids are old enough, they may know which dishes have gotten a good reaction from their parents.

One menu idea is to start with Bruschetta (page 36) and Tomato Topper (page 32) or Caesar Salad (page 46), followed by Tortellini Soup (page 65), with an I Scream Fruit Salad (page 106) for dessert. It's a nice, healthy combination that kids can prepare mostly on their own. The dishes go together well, and they have good appetite appeal for most adults.

Sparkling water in summer or warmed cider in winter make pleasing beverages.

Keep the linens simple, gather a small bouquet of flowers or greenery, and focus on one parent at a time so the other can help with cooking and cleanup.

 # SALADS

What could be easier for—or more satisfying to—a child than tearing up food? It satisfies their natural destructive tendencies (or, should I say, their natural tendencies to take things apart and see what they are made of!?), and makes a very healthful dish: salad!

Many families don't eat enough greens or vegetables. But kids who are accustomed to seeing salads being made usually ask to help with the task (right after they want to help beat eggs!). It looks like fun (tear, tear; cut, cut; shake, shake), and Mom doesn't mind when the kid snacks along the way to the finished dish.

Mozzarella Salad

Skills taught/practiced: slicing, seasoning, presentation.

Ingredients:
  1/4 cup olive oil (more may be needed)
  1/2 tsp. powdered or granulated garlic
    (or more to taste)
  Salt and pepper
  3/4 lb. cherry tomatoes
  1 cup (loosely packed) fresh basil
  3/4 lb. mozzarella (preferably in "cheese stick"
    or "string cheese" form)

1. Measure the olive oil into a bowl big enough to hold all your ingredients. Measure and pour in the garlic powder, and shake in a dash of salt and several dashes of pepper. Stir the seasonings into the oil with a fork or spoon.

2. Remove any stems or leaves from the tomatoes, and rinse the tomatoes in a colander. Take the tomatoes out and put them on a towel to dry.

3. Rinse the basil leaves, too, and pat dry. Tear the basil leaves into dime-sized pieces or smaller, and stir into the oil-and-seasonings mixture. Now, your oil is well-seasoned and will impart great flavor to the other ingredients.

4. Review safe cutting procedures with your child (see pages 20-22). Remove all wrapping from cheese.

Hint: If you have purchased a large block of mozzarella, cut it into bars. That makes it easier for your child to handle (so it doesn't take all day to cut up the cheese).

Using a safe knife, cut the mozzarella sticks into 1/2" chunks, and mix into the olive oil. (The oil moistens the mozzarella and releases more of the cheese's flavor.)

Hint: If you are using fresh mozzarella and the packaging includes a little liquid, pour that into the bowl along with the olive oil for more flavor.

5. When all the cheese is in the bowl, show your child how to use the safe knife to quarter the tomatoes. First cut the tomatoes in half, and then cut the halves in half. Scrape chopped tomatoes into the bowl, and stir all ingredients together. All ingredients should have a light sheen of oil on them. If there doesn't seem to be enough oil, add a little bit at a time.

You can eat this salad immediately, but the flavor will be better if you let the salad marinate at room temperature for at least half an hour.

Variations:
- *You can mix in homemade or store-bought pesto if fresh basil is out of season (this tastes much better than using dried basil).*
- *Add 1/2 cup chopped onions, or 1/4 cup capers, or 1/2 cup chopped black olives (or Tapenade), or 1 cup chopped salad greens (especially red leaf lettuce, watercress, or arugula).*

Fall Feast
(adaptable for Halloween,
Dia de los Muertos, All Saints Day)

It's always comforting to be in the kitchen after the first cold snap of the year; you are no longer competing with the air conditioning whenever you cook! Using your stovetop helps humidify a house desiccated by furnace use, and using your oven only helps warm the house. Plus, the smells of a steamy pot of something yummy simmering warms the heart, too!

For a sit-down feast, you can't go wrong with a big pot of spooky Black Bean Soup (page 71). Start with a Mozzarella Salad (page 40), but try to find orange-fleshed tomatoes. They'll look so good with the black olives (mentioned under *Variations*), that your picky eaters may actually try the salad!

For more portable munching, try a finger-food feast: Quesadillas (page 101) or Flaky Pizzas on page 89 (decorate the tops of either with black olive eyes, green olive noses, and orange-pepper-slice smiles), Bruschetta (page 36) with Tapenade (page 34), Tea Sandwiches (page 86) cut into shapes with Halloween cookie cutters, or Black Bean Dip (page 17) with Homemade "Chips" on page 27 (again, Halloween cookie cutters can make these really great).

Bibb 'n' Orange Salad

Skills taught/practiced: cleaning produce, measuring, seasoning, presentation.

Ingredients:
3 oranges (one for zest/juice, two for sections; get tangelos, if you can find them!)
1/4 cup olive oil
1/4 cup cider vinegar
1 Tbsp. teriyaki sauce (optional)
1/4 cup (or more) chopped almonds (optional)
1 head of Bibb lettuce
Salt and pepper

1. In this recipe, you'll make the dressing in the bowl, and then stir the lettuce pieces into it. Begin by washing the oranges.

2. Show your child/ren how to zest an orange, and zest one of them completely, letting the zest fall into your salad bowl.

3. Then juice that orange completely, letting the juice fall into the bowl. Use a strainer to catch the seeds, or let the kids have fun fishing them out.

4. Measure in the olive oil and cider vinegar, and teriyaki, if you have it. This is optional.

5. Begin peeling an orange for your kids (if they can't "start" an orange) and let them finish it. Put peeled, sectioned orange pieces into the bowl. If the

pieces are bigger than bite-sized, review safe knife techniques and show your child/ren how to use a safe knife to cut the sections into bite-sized pieces (see pages 20-22).

6. Measure in the chopped almonds and stir the dressing.

7. Cut the stem end out of the lettuce head and rinse the leaves. Tear into bite-sized pieces and put in bowl.

8. Mix salad, and serve.

Variations:

- *You could tear lettuce leaves into another bowl and pour the dressing on top.*
- *Balsamic vinegar gives this salad a great taste. If you use it, you can probably use half as much vinegar as the recipe calls for, and you won't need the teriyaki sauce.*
- *You can use two cans of mandarin oranges if you can't find decent fresh oranges where you live, or if your kids are intensely anti-pith (pith being the white strings and membrane on the outside of a peeled orange). In that case, you can use the juice from the cans in the dressing.*
- *Fresh grapefruit juice and sections also work well in this recipe, if you have grapefruit-eaters in your house.*

Cucumber Moon Salad

Skills taught/practiced:
cleaning produce, measuring, seasoning, presentation.

Ingredients:
2 cucumbers
¼ cup white vinegar (approximately)
Salt and pepper

1. Peel the cucumbers and cut off the tops and bottoms.

2. Slice in half lengthwise, cut 1/4" slices from each half (which should look like little half moons), and scrape into flat-bottomed dish.

3. Pour in enough vinegar to cover the cucumber moons, and add salt and pepper to taste. Stir the cucumber moons around, and salt lightly again if necessary.

4. Cover the dish and chill. You can serve this like a pickle alongside anything that needs a slightly sour accompaniment: hot dogs or bratwurst, potato salad or fried chicken, or toss it with a mixed green salad.

Variations:

- *I like to use rice wine vinegar in this recipe; it gives the best flavor, I think.*
- *You can use white pepper or no pepper at all if you don't want your cucumber moons pocked by black dots.*
- *If you scrape the seeds out (use a teaspoon or grapefruit spoon), you'll have crescent moons!*

Caesar Salad

Skills taught/practiced:
cleaning produce, measuring, seasoning, presentation.

Ingredients:
1 head of romaine lettuce
½ cup milk
½ tsp. Thai fish sauce
or 1 tsp. powdered garlic
1 lemon
1 cup mayonnaise
1 cup grated Parmesan *or* Romano cheese
(divided use)
Salt and pepper

1. Help your child use his or her safe knife (a lightly serrated butter or table knife) to cut the bottom off the head of romaine (see pages 20-22).

2. Compost the bottom and any outer leaves that have gotten yucky, and rinse the rest of the leaves in the sink. (My kids love playing with water in the sink, so this is a favorite task.)

3. Wrap the leaves in paper or cloth toweling and set aside in the fridge (so you won't be in a hurry) while assembling the dressing.

4. You can make the dressing by shaking it in a jar or by whirling it in a blender. I like the jar because kids like shaking, it's safer for them than a blender, and I

don't like how much dressing gets left behind in the blender. Your child/ren could also whisk the ingredients in a bowl. Measure the milk in first to keep the mayonnaise from clinging stubbornly to the bottom of the jar.

5. Measure in and add the fish sauce, if you have it on hand. Don't buy a bottle just for this recipe. It'll give just the slightest hint of the anchovy taste found in a really traditional Caesar. (Very slight. I don't like anchovies, but I like this little touch of flavor in the dressing.) If you don't have—or doubt the value of— fish sauce, add the powdered garlic to prevent a totally bland dressing.

6. Add the juice of one lemon; this is a great time to show your kids how to use a citrus reamer.

7. Add the mayonnaise a few spoonfuls at a time, and either shake it up in the jar or whisk it together in the bowl. Keep adding mayonnaise until the dressing is the consistency your kids like. The amounts in this recipe are imprecise to allow you and your child/ren to find the consistency you prefer. So this is a great time to talk about adjusting ingredient amounts to suit yourself.

8. Mix 1/4 cup shredded or grated Parmesan into the dressing. Add salt and pepper to taste and it's done. Refrigerate until time to serve.

9. When you're ready to serve the salad, get little fingers busy tearing romaine into bite-sized pieces. Put the pieces into a big salad bowl with extra room for tossing.

10. Pour some dressing over the romaine, sprinkle on a little salt and a lot of pepper, and stir with big spoons. Turn the leaves over and over. If there is not enough dressing to coat all leaves, add some more. When the salad has enough dressing, sprinkle the rest of the grated Parmesan or Romano over the top, and serve.

Variations:

- *Add 1-2 tsp. lemon juice to the dressing instead of the fish sauce.*
- *If you have bread around that's going stale, make croutons. Cut or tear the bread into 1/2-inch cube-ish shapes. Spray with butter or olive oil cooking spray, sprinkle with garlic powder, and toast in the oven. Sprinkle over the top liberally. These croutons will taste much better and are much healthier than store-bought ones.*
- *If you have leftover chicken, cut it into bite-sized pieces, and serve on the side or mixed into the salad.*

Greek Salad

Skills taught/practiced:
cleaning produce, measuring, seasoning, presentation.

Ingredients:

1/2 lb. block of feta cheese

2 lemons

4-5 sprigs fresh parsley
(omit if fresh is not available)

4-5 sprigs fresh oregano (use 2 teaspoons
dried if fresh is not available)

2 cloves of garlic

1/2 cup olive oil

1 cup black olives

2 stalks of celery

2 sweet bell peppers (preferably one yellow
and one red)

1 large *or* 2 small cucumbers

1/2 lb. cherry tomatoes

1 head of romaine (if making a salad)

1. Crumble the feta cheese into a bowl big enough to hold all ingredients (except the romaine). *Note*: Feta cheese usually comes stored in a plastic pouch or container with some liquid inside. I usually pour the liquid into the bowl with the cheese. Ask your child to use clean fingers or a fork to crumble the feta into pea-sized pieces. Measure and pour in the olive oil.

2. If you have time, show your child how to zest the lemons before reaming; it's optional, but a nice addition. Then show your child how to ream the lemons, and then pour the juice through a strainer into the bowl.

3. If using fresh herbs, rinse and then tear the leaves off. Put pea-sized or smaller leaves into the bowl, and cut the rest up into little pieces and put into the bowl. If using dried oregano, show your child/ren how to measure the appropriate amount and crumble into the bowl by rubbing between the palms of his or her hands.

4. Separate several cloves from the garlic head.

Note: An adult should cut off the top and bottom edges of each clove. A child or an adult can smash the clove: put the clove under something heavy like a metal spatula, and then bang down on it with your fist. Splat! goes the clove. Now a child can pick the garlic meat out of the papery husk and cut the meat into finer bits with a safe knife. Put into bowl. Add the olive oil.

5. Use a safe knife to cut the olives into pea-sized pieces (see pages 20-22). Add to the bowl. Stir once or twice, but not enough to blend the ingredients. (Putting these ingredients in first helps the flavor.)

6. Trim the celery ends and tops (put in stock bag). Next, cut the celery stalks in half lengthwise. Line the halved lengths up together and cut across into 1/4" dice. The ends, being wider, may need additional chopping. Scrape celery into bowl.

7. Cut off the bell pepper tops and take out the seed pod at the top. (You can chop up the tops for soup, or put the tops into the stock bag. Discard the stem and seed pod, or put in compost bowl.) Cut peppers into strips. Cut the strips into 1/4" dice and scrape into bowl.

8. Peel the cucumbers and cut off the tops and bottoms. Slice in half lengthwise. Use a teaspoon or grapefruit spoon to scrape out the seeds. Cut meat into pea- or bean-sized chunks and scrape into bowl.

9. Show your child how to use a safe knife to quarter the tomatoes. First cut the tomatoes in half, and then cut the halves in half. (You may need to cut the tomatoes into more pieces than quarters; you want to produce bean-sized pieces. But bigger chunks are okay if that's what your child can accomplish.) Scrape chopped tomatoes into the bowl and stir all ingredients together.

Note: The salad will taste best if you let these ingredients marinate in the fridge for an hour or so. This mixture will keep for several days, though the soft ingredients, like cucumbers and tomatoes, get mushier as the days go by.

10. When you are ready to serve the salad, cut off the bottom of the romaine and tear off any yucky leaves for compost. Rinse the romaine, tear into bite-sized pieces, and put the pieces into a big salad bowl.

11. Pour the vegetable mixture on top and season to taste with salt and pepper. You can either serve it like

this, or stir everything up together. Garnish with a couple of sprigs of parsley or oregano, or with lemon slices.

Variations:
- *This mixture (sans romaine) is nice on pasta, rice, or baked potatoes.*
- *You can also serve a mound of it alongside some baked or grilled chicken (especially if the chicken was treated to a lemon/oregano/olive oil marinade).*

SOUPS

Soup is another kind of food that's great for kids. It's hard to mess up, really healthy to eat, it can be a meal in itself, or it can accompany other dishes.

If this book landed in your hands in summertime, and soup is the last thing on your mind, don't skip this section too quickly. The recipes for Pink Soup and Gazpacho can be served cool and are both quite refreshing. And Nan's Gazpacho doesn't require any cooking at all!

Of course, any season is a good time to add to your stock bag. What's a stock bag, you might ask? It's the secret behind the one key to easy, economical, and excellent soup-making:

Happy Cook Principle 4:

Make soup stock from scratch and you'll have meals in minutes for months!

SOUPS

This is just too easy and important a step to skip, so I tell you below how to make three different stocks: vegetable/vegetarian, chicken/turkey, and beef stock.

In *A Guide to Happy Family Gardening*, I mentioned how easy it was to build a compost supply from fruit and vegetable scraps. But there are a few kitchen scraps that never find their way into my compost bowl. These go into a bag in the freezer that saves up ingredients for stock-making: celery ends and leafy tops, onion and garlic husks and ends, potato and carrot skins, carrot ends and leafy tops, zucchini ends, chicken or turkey bones, beef bones—anything that'll add flavor to the stock should go into your freezer bags.

So while you are accumulating your stock ingredients, start with a quick bowl of Nan's Gazpacho (opposite) or a pretty tureen of Pink Soup (but save the scraps from Pink Soup's secret ingredient found on page 58; they're good for stock-making!).

Nan's Gazpacho

Skills taught/practiced: cutting, seasoning.

Ingredients:
1 Tbsp. Worcestershire sauce
1 tsp. sugar
1 Tbsp. olive oil
Dash salt and pepper
1/4 cup cilantro leaves, chopped fine
Juice from one lime *or* lemon
3-4 ripe tomatoes
1 cucumber
2-3 stalks of celery
2 green bell peppers
2-3 green onions
  (optional; serve on side if preferred)

1. Measure Worcestershire sauce, sugar, olive oil, salt, and pepper into bowl big enough to hold all ingredients.

2. Chop and add cilantro leaves (put stems in stock bag).

3. Use a reamer to juice lime or lemon into the bowl.

4. Whisk ingredients together and set aside. *Note*: Mixing these ingredients into the bowl first helps the flavors meld, and the dressing serves as a marinade for the other ingredients. Following this sequence also

keeps you from having to stir the other ingredients excessively.

5. Use a safe knife to chop the tomatoes (see pages 20-22). If using large tomatoes (i.e., larger than cherry tomatoes), an adult may want to first cut the stem area out, or slice the top off if it is fairly flat. Then a child can cut the tomatoes in half, and in half again. Bigger chunks are okay if that's what your child can accomplish; you can chop them a little finer if necessary. Scrape chopped tomatoes and their juice into the bowl with the dressing ingredients.

6. Trim the cucumber ends with the safe knife. Show your child how to use a vegetable peeler to take the green skin off the cucumber, or a fork to score the skin. (Frankly, this is hard for me and may be beyond a child's ability, but they may find it interesting to see how this technique works and what effect it produces.) Use the safe knife to cut the cucumber in half lengthwise. Use a teaspoon to scrape out the seeds. Then use the safe knife again to cut the cucumber into small pieces (similar to the size you cut the tomato).

7. Trim the celery ends and tops (put in stock bag). Next, cut the celery stalks in half lengthwise. Line the halved lengths up together and cut across into ¼" dice. The ends, being wider, may need additional chopping. Scrape celery into bowl.

8. Cut off the bell pepper tops and take out the seed pod at the top. (You can chop up the tops for soup, or

put the tops into the stock bag. Discard the stem and seed pod, or put in compost bowl.

Cut peppers into strips. Cut the strips into 1/4" dice and scrape into bowl.

9. An adult should chop the onions to prevent child/ren from getting onion juice in their eyes. You may want to serve the onions on the side so kids can try just a little bit at first.

10. Mix all other ingredients and refrigerate for an hour before serving. This soup is best served cold, garnished with fresh cilantro. For fun on a hot day, serve in chilled bowls!

Variations:

- *Serve fat-free sour cream or yogurt on the side. It's not traditional, but some people like to stir in a dollop.*
- *Adults (and heat-tolerant kids) may like hot peppers in this dish. If so, an adult should chop these and serve them on the side. Try jalapenos, serranos, or habaneros—whatever you have on hand, or whatever you know your chili-head family members or friends like.*

Pink Soup

Skills taught/practiced: cutting, seasoning, boiling.

Ingredients:
   6-8 cups water
   3-4 beets (fresh, not canned)
   1/2 tsp. sugar
   1/4 tsp. salt (or more to taste)
   1/4 tsp. pepper (or more to taste)
   1 cup plain or vanilla yogurt, *or* sour cream

1. Review rules for safe usage of stovetop burners (see pages 66-67). Get a pot big enough to hold all the beets, and still have some room left at the top. Fill with enough water to cover all the beets by two inches, and turn on the heat to bring the water to boil.

2. An adult should trim the greens and roots off the beets, peel the skin off (these can go in the stock bag), and cut each beet in half so it will lie flat on the cutting board. (*Note*: An adult can prepare this recipe in advance up to this stage to prevent kid boredom.)

3. Depending on how firm the beets are, a child should be able to cut each beet half in half again, and continue cutting each chunk until all the beet pieces are about the size of a walnut or pecan. Or, you may want to boil the beets and then cut them (be prepared for a lot of pink surfaces, including hands!) so they will be softer and easier to work with.

4. Put the beets in the large pot with boiling water and cook until tender. **You will want to reserve the cooking liquid for later, so do not pour beets out into a strainer**. Take beets out with a slotted spoon and put into a bowl to cool (preferably a non-stainable bowl, like stainless steel). You may want to show your kids that the water is now quite pink! Amazing.

5. Smash cooled beets with a fork or potato masher or ricer. Again, take care to use tools and work on surfaces that will not stain, or that you don't mind turning pink.

6. Put the smashed beets into another cooking pot (or the same one if you have stored the beet cooking water elsewhere, like a glass jar) with some of the cooking water. Stir the beets and cooking water together with a whisk or slotted spoon to make a puree.

Alternate method: An adult can use a blender, hand-held blender, or food processor to puree the beets with a little of the cooking water.

7. Toward the end of the pureeing process, add the sugar, salt, pepper, and 1/4 cup yogurt (or sour cream). After you finish pureeing all the beets, check —and, if necessary, correct—the consistency of the soup. If it is more like mashed potatoes than soup, add more water. If the soup is too watery, cook some of the water out by simmering gently on the stove (check seasonings; you may need more after cooking the water out), or add a couple of spoonfuls of potato flakes.

8. Ladle the soup into pretty bowls (clear or white are beautiful), and stir in a spoonful of yogurt or sour cream, using the spoon to make a swirl.

Variations:
- *The most important variation is to cook the beets in vegetable or chicken stock. This will add much more flavor.*
- *Add a tablespoonful of cider vinegar or rice wine vinegar to the pot before serving if you want a more tart taste.*
- *Garnish with mint, if you have fresh.*
- *Another pretty garnish is to boil eggs in the beet water, if you have any left. It will dye them a lovely pink. If you peel the eggs, and they don't look pink on the inside, let them sit in the beet water for a while. Then you can slice them and serve a slice on top of each bowl of soup. The yellow and white rings look attractive on the Pink Soup.*

Valentine's for Two
(or Twenty)

How about Tea Sandwiches (page 86) or Quesadillas (page 101) trimmed into heart shapes? Serve with Pink Soup (page 58), of course, perhaps accompanied by Strawberry Smoothies (blend 1 cup strawberry yogurt, one very cold or frozen banana, and 3-4 very cold or frozen strawberries. Pour into 2 chilled glasses and serve).

Decorate the table with lots of homemade Valentine hearts made of red construction paper and doilies, and use red and white or silver tableware and linens. For dessert, well, what could be better than a decadent Very Chocolate Cherry Cake (page 109) cooked in a heart-shaped pan?

Making Stock

Skills taught/practiced:
cutting, seasoning, boiling, fat-skimming.

Ingredients:
Whatever you've stored in your freezer bags:
   vegetable scraps, bones, etc.
Water
or
4 small *or* 2 big potatoes
4 carrots
4 stems of celery (include leaves)
4 small *or* 2 big onions
4 garlic cloves
4 tsp. black peppercorns
Handful of herbs (whatever you've got:
   bay leaf, oregano, parsley, rosemary, basil,
   a couple of whole cloves)
Water

For Vegetable Stock

You will get a richer result if you first brown the chopped or sliced onions in the pot in a bit of olive oil or butter.

If using stock-bag scraps, dump them into the pot.

If using the vegetables listed above, coarsely cut them into chunks. (An adult should cut up the onion and may want to cut potatoes and carrots in half to prevent them from rolling around when the child/ren works to chunk them with a safe knife.) Cover stock ingredients with water. (Some stock ingredients may float. This is okay; just be sure there is plenty of water to cover.) Bring to a boil, partially cover with a lid, and lower temperature to a simmer.

For Chicken Stock

To your stock-bag scraps, or to the vegetables listed above, add 2 pounds of saved chicken scraps, or purchase and add cheap chicken parts (backs, wings, thighs, legs), or use all the bones from your Thanksgiving turkey (which makes it turkey stock, of course). Add water to cover.

Bring to a boil and simmer at least an hour. Longer simmering will produce a better flavor.

For Beef Stock

To give the stock a much richer flavor (be sure to review safe oven practices on pages 30-31), put 2 pounds of meaty beef in a roasting pan and roast them in a 450°F. oven for half an hour. Ask your butcher for these bones; you may have to pay for them.

Get out a pot big enough to hold all your ingredients, with 3 inches of space left at the top. Review rules for safe usage of stovetop burners (pages 66-67).

If using stock-bag scraps, dump them into the pot. If using the vegetables listed above, coarsely chop them, following instructions under "For Vegetable Stock."

Cover with water and bring to a boil, partially cover with a lid, and lower temperature to a simmer. Add roasted bones to the simmering stockpot, along with pan drippings and crusty bits, and simmer for three hours. (Beef bones can be put in raw, but this means you need to simmer longer: at least four hours.)

When the stock is done simmering, use a slotted spoon to take out the largest solids. Then pour the stock through a colander or strainer into a bowl.

Refrigerate until stock gels. The fat will rise to the top of the bowl where you can skim it off with a slotted spoon or spatula.

Use the stock immediately, or freeze it for later.

Hint: Use a measuring cup to ladle stock into freezer bags or containers. Label with amount stored in the bag before freezing.

Tortellini Soup

Skills taught/practiced: seasoning and simmering.

Ingredients:
6 cups stock (preferably beef,
    but chicken and vegetable work fine)
2 packages refrigerated or frozen cheese
    tortellini (other fillings are fine)
1 10- *or* 17-oz. can canned tomato pieces
    (plain *or* Italian-seasoned)
1 tsp. powdered garlic
Pinch salt and pepper

1. Review the rules for safe stovetop use (pages 66-67). Put stock in a pot big enough to hold all ingredients, and bring stock to a boil. When the stock is boiling, pour in the tortellini and cook according to package directions. (Usually when they float, it is time to fish one out and test for doneness.)

2. *Note*: An adult should open the can of tomatoes, so that the child does not have to use a sharp can opener, or risk injury on the sharp edge of the can. Be sure to show your child how to avoid the can edges when using a spoon to scoop the tomatoes into the pot.

3. After five minutes of cooking the tortellini, add the tomatoes and bring the soup back to a simmer.

4. Measure and pour in the garlic powder, salt, and

pepper. When tortellini are done and tomatoes are warmed through, soup is ready to serve.

Variations:
- *Break a piece of dried-out or stale bread into each bowl before pouring in soup.*
- *Top with grated Parmesan or Romano cheese.*
- *Garnish with shredded fresh basil.*

Safe Stovetop, Safe Cook

Before using the stovetop the first time, please go over safe usage practices with your child/ren. You know your child, your utensils, and your stove better than I do, and there is no way I can envision every situation. So let me just provide some pointers:

- Teach your child/ren how to turn a stove on and off safely. If you don't want to teach them to turn it on yet, consider teaching them to turn it off. The day may come when you need them to do that, when you have your hands full with something else.

- Teach your child/ren what "hot" means: hold their hands and get close enough to a safe source of heat to feel the "hot." As something cooks, explain that the same thing can happen to us if we get too close to the heat. Explain that a burn accident can happen even if we are being very careful, and that heat and flame are not something to fool around with.

- Teach your child/ren to work "remotely," i.e., using something other than their hands to manipulate foods, such as long-handled spoons and tongs. Remember that wooden ones can be very lightweight, versatile, and plenty strong. This extends to always using hotpads when approaching or picking up a pan or a pot.

- Teach your child/ren to keep a safe distance from a pot when the heat is on, especially when the pot is boiling or when the cook is lifting a lid. The escaping steam can scald.

And remember: Be sure your child knows to never, ever use a stovetop without an adult supervising.

Nacho Soup

Skills taught/practiced: grating, seasoning, warming.

Ingredients:
4 cups stock (vegetable, chicken, or beef)
2 16-oz. cans refried beans
   or 2 16-oz. cans pinto beans*
1 tsp. powdered garlic
2 tsp. cumin
Pinch salt and pepper
1 large bag tortilla chips
2 cups cheese (Monterey Jack, Colby Jack, *or* cheddar)

1. Review rules for safe stovetop usage (see pages 66-67). Put stock in a pot big enough to hold all ingredients, and set on medium heat to begin warming the stock.

*If using pinto beans, pour any liquid in the can into the pot and scoop beans onto a plate for smashing. Scrape smashed beans into stockpot.

2. *Note*: An adult should open the cans of beans, so that the child does not have to use a sharp can opener, or risk injury on the sharp edge of the cans. Be sure to show your child how to avoid the can edges when using a spoon to scoop the beans into the pot.

3. Measure and pour in the garlic powder, cumin, salt, and pepper. Use a slotted spoon or fork to stir the soup,

pressing the chunks of beans up against the side of the pot so they become incorporated with the stock.

4. While the soup is warming, put 4-5 chips in each soup bowl. Grate the cheese (if it is not already shredded) and put a loose ¼ cup in each bowl.

5. When the soup is steaming warm (it doesn't need to come to a boil, but a brief simmer will help meld flavors), pour into bowl on top of chips, cheese, and any other desired ingredients (see Variations), and serve.

Variations:

- *You can put anything into this soup that you would put on nachos: chicken chunks, a dollop of sour cream, tomato or avocado pieces, chopped onions.*
- *Garnish with a few pieces of the grated cheese and one chip stuck in standing up, or any of the Variation extras.*

Moveable Feasts and Gastronomic Acts of Kindness

Planning a potluck, a picnic, a tailgate party? Sharing with a soup kitchen or another group? While soup can be hard to transport, Tortellini Soup (page 65) does offer an interesting option. If there is a stove at your serving location, you can transport most of the ingredients to the location and cook it there. I once went to a Christmas party and took 20 2-cup bags of frozen homemade stock, 10 packages of tortellini, and 10 cans of Italian-seasoned canned tomato pieces. There was some good-natured laughter as I arrived heavily laden, but the laughter turned to "Mmm-mmm . . . now how did you make this?" before too long.

Nacho Soup (page 68) is another that is easy to make in quantity since the number of ingredients is small. Quesadillas (page 101) can be made ahead and reheated in an oven or microwave when it's time to serve. Tea Sandwiches (page 86) can be prepared ahead and kept cool. Cucumber Moon Salad (page 45) gets better the longer it waits, as does Mozzarella Salad (page 40). Both are easy to make in large quantities, as is Fruit Salad (page 106). For a family with sick members, or who have experienced a death in the family, these are especially flexible gifts to offer, and they provide healthy nutrients to stressed-out bodies.

Black Bean Soup

Skills taught/practiced: grating, seasoning, simmering.

Ingredients:
4 cups stock (vegetable, chicken, or beef)
16-oz. can of black beans
1/2 tsp. powdered garlic
1 tsp. cumin
Pinch salt and pepper
2 large *or* 4 small tomatoes
1 cup kernel corn (preferably frozen)

1. Review rules for safe stovetop usage (pages 66-67). Put stock in a pot big enough to hold all ingredients, and set on medium heat to begin warming the stock.

2. *Note*: An adult should open the can of beans, so that the child does not have to use a sharp can opener, or risk injury on the sharp edge of the can. Be sure to show your child how to avoid the can edges when using a spoon to scoop the beans into the pot. Stir in the beans (leave them whole; do not smash them), including any liquid in the can.

3. Measure and pour in the garlic powder, cumin, salt, and pepper.

4. While the soup is warming, show your child how to use a safe knife to quarter the tomatoes. First, cut the tomatoes in half, and then cut the halves in half. Scrape chopped tomatoes into the bowl.

5. Pour in the corn and bring the soup to a simmer. Simmer for five minutes, and then pour the soup into a bowl with any other desired ingredients (see Variations), and serve.

Variations:

- *You can add bite-sized chicken, a dollop of sour cream or yogurt, avocado pieces, or chopped onions.*
- *Add chips and cheese as with Nacho Soup, if desired (see page 68).*

Turkey & Corn Chowder

Skills taught/practiced:
cutting, sautéing, measuring, seasoning, simmering.

Ingredients:
1 Tbsp. butter, margarine *or* olive oil
1 onion
2 ribs celery
1 green bell pepper
2 carrots
4 cups stock (vegetable, chicken, *or* beef,
    but preferably turkey)
2 potatoes
3 cups cooked, diced turkey
1 17-oz. can creamed corn
2 cups milk (skim *or* reduced fat)
1/4 cup fresh herbs
    (basil, oregano, flat leaf parsley)
Salt and pepper

1. Review rules for safe stovetop use (see pages 66-67). In a pot big enough to hold all the ingredients, melt the butter or margarine, or pour in the olive oil.

2. An adult should chop the onion to prevent child/ren from getting onion juice in their eyes. Sauté the onions while cutting up celery and pepper.

3. Trim the celery ends and tops (put in stock bag). Next, a child can use a safe knife to cut the celery

stalks in half lengthwise. Show your child how to line the halved lengths up together and cut across into ¼" dice. The ends, being wider, may need additional chopping. Scrape celery into pot and continue the sauté.

4. Cut off the bell pepper tops and take out the seed pod at the top. (You can chop up the tops for the soup, or put the tops into the stock bag. Discard the stem and seed pod, or put in compost bowl.) Cut peppers into strips. Cut the strips into ¼" dice, and scrape into pot and continue the sauté.

5. An adult should cut the carrots in half lengthwise so they don't roll. A child can then use a safe knife to cut the carrots into bite-sized chunks.

6. Put the carrots in the pot and add the stock. Bring to a light boil, and let simmer for five minutes.

7. While the carrots simmer, cut up the potatoes. An adult should cut the potatoes in half lengthwise so they don't roll. A child can then use a safe knife to cut the potatoes into bite-sized chunks.

8. Put the potatoes in the pot, add the turkey, and bring back to a light boil. Let the soup simmer for 10 minutes, or until the potatoes and carrots are tender.

9. While the soup simmers, measure out the corn, milk, and seasonings. When the vegetables are tender and the turkey is warmed through, add the corn, milk, herbs, salt, and pepper.

10. When you are ready to serve, warm the soup through again, but don't let it come to a boil.

Variations:

- *If you don't have turkey stock, use chicken stock. If you don't have turkey meat, use chicken meat.*
- *For a vegetarian chowder, use vegetable stock. Replace the turkey with 2 cups of cooked brown rice (and 1 cup of wild rice for a really special touch). Add chopped tomatoes and zucchini with the milk and corn.*
- *Skip the milk and creamed corn if you don't like a creamy soup. Just add more stock and use an equal amount of frozen corn kernels. Add frozen corn with potatoes and turkey.*

Thanksgiving/Christmas/ Winter Festivities

You may want to take a slightly different tack some years with one of the big winter holidays, and help the kids make the feast instead of them helping you.

At Thanksgiving, or at any other holiday time, you just can't go wrong with a big steaming pot of Turkey and Corn Chowder (page 73). In November this soup gives you a chance to talk about the first Thanksgiving, and you can include any chunks of pumpkin you may happen to have around! They'll mix in quite nicely; just add a little extra stock at cooking time.

On the other hand, if you make a conventional Thanksgiving feast, you can get a big headstart toward making the Chowder for Christmas or for another winter feast. Save the turkey carcass and any leftover meat. Freeze the edible meat in the right size chunks for the soup, and make stock from the turkey carcass. If you had corn on the cob, cut corn off any leftover cobs and freeze for later.

Precede the soup by a nice Caesar (page 46) or Bibb 'n' Orange Salad (page 43) for a light but satisfying meal, and you'll still have room for Chocolate Cake (page 109) or Apple Crumble (page 112).

Tortilla Soup

Skills taught/practiced:
cutting, grating, sautéing, seasoning, simmering.

Ingredients:
- 1 Tbsp. butter, margarine, *or* olive oil
- 1 onion
- 2 ribs celery
- 1 green bell pepper
- 2 carrots
- 3 cups stock (vegetable or chicken)
- 1 zucchini
- 10-12 cherry tomatoes
- 2 cups kernel corn (preferably frozen)
- 1 tsp. cumin
- 1 tsp. powdered garlic
- Salt and pepper
- 1 pound Monterey Jack *or* Colby Jack cheese
- ½ cup chopped cilantro
- Tortilla chips

1. Review rules for safe stovetop use (see pages 66-67). In a pot big enough to hold all the ingredients, melt the butter or margarine, or pour in the olive oil.

2. An adult should chop the onions to prevent child/ren from getting onion juice in their eyes. Sauté the onions while cutting up celery and pepper.

SOUPS

---

3. Trim the celery ends and tops (put in stock bag). Next, cut the celery stalks in half lengthwise. Line the halved lengths up together and cut across into 1/4" dice. The ends, being wider, may need additional chopping. Scrape celery into pot and continue the sauté.

4. Cut off the bell pepper tops and take out the seed pod at the top. (You can chop up the tops for the soup, or put the tops into the stock bag. But discard the stem and seed pod, or put in compost bowl.) Cut peppers into strips. Cut the strips into 1/4" dice, scrape into pot, and continue the sauté.

5. An adult should cut the carrots in half lengthwise so they don't roll. A child can then use a safe knife to cut the carrots into bite-sized chunks.

6. Put the carrots in the pot and add the stock. Bring to a light boil and let simmer for five minutes.

7. While the soup is simmering, an adult should cut the zucchini in half lengthwise. A child can then use a

safe knife to cut the half in half again lengthwise, and then cut the zucchini strips into bite-size chunks (or smaller). Add the zucchini to the soup and bring back to a simmer.

8. Use the same serrated table knife and show your child how to quarter the tomatoes. First cut the tomatoes in half, and then cut the halves in half. (You may need to cut the tomatoes in more pieces than quarters; you want to produce bean-sized pieces. But bigger chunks are okay if that's what your child can accomplish.)

9. Scrape chopped tomatoes into the pot along with corn, cumin, powdered garlic, salt, and pepper. Bring the soup back to a simmer.

10. Grate cheese if it isn't already shredded. Cut cilantro into small pieces. Put tortilla chips, cheese, and cilantro in each bowl.

11. When the zucchini is tender, ladle the soup into bowls and serve.

Variations:
- *Add 2 cups cooked, diced chicken.*
- *Add 1 tsp. salsa to each bowl.*

# ENTRÉES

There's something for everyone in this section: sandwiches and pizzas and pasta salads. All of them are colorful, tasty, and well within the reach of most kids who can at least participate in preparing them. Younger kids may need some help with all the chopping in recipes like Confetti Alphabetti, but you'll both like the results so much, it'll be worth it!

The Quesadilla recipe is easy to make with very little prep, but it does include warming or grilling tortillas on a hot surface. So think carefully about what little hands are able to do, and what you need to do for them.

When you think your child/ren are ready to handle the hot stuff, try a dry run with cold tortillas and a cold griddle. Get the technique down, and then turn on the stove.

Which Came First? Salad
(aka Chicken & Egg Salad)

Skills taught/practiced:
cleaning produce, measuring, seasoning, presentation.

Ingredients:
2 large eggs *or* 3 small
1 head leaf lettuce
1/2 cup mayonnaise
    (you may not use all of this)
2 Tbsp. prepared mustard
    (whatever variety your family likes)
1/4 tsp. dried, minced onion,
    or use 1 Tbsp. fresh, if you prefer
1/4 tsp. powdered garlic
    or 1/4 tsp. curry powder
2 ribs celery
1 10-oz. can chunk chicken

1. Review safe stovetop (pages 66-67) and knife usage (pages 20-22). Put eggs in pot of water (enough to cover the eggs) on the stove and bring to boil. (You could drop them into boiling water, but that tends to crack the shell and let egg leak out into the water. It'll get cooked anyway, but it makes a mess.)

When the water boils, set the timer for 9-10 minutes.

2. If you will serve the salad immediately after preparing it, go ahead and get the lettuce ready (oth-

erwise, wait until you *are* ready to serve). Cut off bottom of lettuce head and clean leaves, discarding or composting yucky leaves.

Tear lettuce leaves into bite-sized pieces and put into one large bowl, or four individual serving bowls. Set aside.

3. While eggs are cooking, put ¼ cup or ⅓ cup mayonnaise into a bowl and add mustard, minced onion, and powdered garlic. Mix and set aside.

4. Trim the celery ends and tops (put in stock bag). Next, a child can use a safe knife to cut the celery stalks in half lengthwise. Show your child how to line the halved lengths up together and cut across the ¼" dice. The ends, being wider, may need additional chopping. Add the chopped celery to the bowl.

5. *Note*: An adult should open the can of chicken, so that the child does not have to use a sharp can opener, or risk injury on the sharp edge of the can. Be sure to show your child how to avoid the can edges when using a spoon to scoop out the chicken. Use fingers to shred the chicken to a point where there are still bite-sized chunks. Add to bowl.

6. When eggs are done, take out of water and let cool until they can be handled. (Sometimes I put the eggs in a bowl of water with ice cubes to help this process along.) Lightly tap the egg all over and peel.

7. Now you want to chop the eggs into bean- or pea-sized dice. I have a wire egg slicer gizmo that folds down over the egg and helps with this very nicely. If

you don't have one, just slice and reslice the eggs with a safe knife.

8. Mix egg and chicken into the seasoned mayonnaise. If the salad is too dry for you, add more mayo one teaspoon at a time until the consistency is right for you.

9. Spoon over lettuce and serve. Or, serve on toasted wheat bread with lettuce for sandwiches.

Variations:

- *I usually make double this recipe since my family loves chicken/egg salad, but this recipe will make enough for four generous salad servings or sandwiches.*
- *You can use an equal amount of plain yogurt instead of mayonnaise.*
- *You can add 1/2 cup chopped walnuts or 1/2 cup chopped almonds or 1 small apple (cored and chopped into bean-sized pieces) or 1/2 cup raisins or 1/2 cup grapes (sliced in half or quarters; easy for a kid to do).*

Beyond Balloons:
Happy Birthday!

I think it's too bad that most kids only get to wear their Halloween costumes at Halloween. How about a costume party for your child/ren's birthday? Advise all guests to wear their favorite costume, or make one up. (You may want to have one or two extra costumes on hand for kids—who want one—who show up without one.) Provide greasepaint crayons, and kids can paint faces as they arrive. Now you're ready!

For an entertaining lunch that's more fun than Floppy the Clown, how about a salad and sandwich bar? Provide salad and sandwich fixin's and let your guests—large or small—get busy building their own. You can carry the theme forward to dessert by serving ice cream and homemade cookies that the guests can smoosh into cookie-ice cream sundaes.

Tea Sandwiches

Skills taught/practiced:
spreading, slicing, mixing, presentation.

Ingredients (*Note:* these depend on which sandwiches you decide to make, so you probably want to draw up your own list, but here are some ideas):
  1-2 loaves bread (white, wheat *or* both)
  1 jar peanut butter
  1 or more jars jelly (one *or* several kinds)
  1 container marshmallow fluff
  8-oz. thin-sliced lunch meat
      (ham, roast beef, turkey, *or* all three)
  1 package thin-sliced cheese
  1 bunch small tomatoes
  1 jar of English pickle
      (10-oz. will last forever; see page 88)
  1 batch Chicken & Egg Salad (see page 82)
  1 head lettuce
  1 package whipped *or* soft-spread cream cheese
  1 cucumber

Peanut-Butter-Jelly (PBJ) sandwiches:
  1. Review safe knife usage (pages 20-22) before beginning. You may want to use white bread for color contrast. Spread a thin coat of peanut butter on one side of one piece of bread, and a thin smear of jelly on one side of another piece of bread.

2. Put together, slice off crusts, cut across the sandwich on the diagonal to make two sandwich triangles, and lay aside under a damp paper towel. (Save crusts in a bag to feed birds later, especially if you live near an area where they congregate.)

Fluffer-Nutter Sandwiches:

1. Review safe knife usage (pages 20-22) before beginning. Use marshmallow fluff instead of jelly, and use whole wheat bread for color contrast.

2. Repeat steps for making PBJ Sandwiches above.

Ham-and-Cheese Sandwiches (or roast-beef and cheese, or turkey and cheese):

1. Review safe knife usage (pages 20-22) before beginning. Spread the bread with mayo or mustard and use thin slices of ham and your favorite cheese. (Sharp cheddar goes nicely with roast beef, mild cheddar or American cheese with ham, and provolone with turkey).

2. Again, cut crusts off and cut sandwiches on the diagonal. Set aside under a damp paper towel.

Cheese and Tomato Sandwiches:

A visit to England inspired me to try Cheese and Tomato Sandwiches: a thin smear of mayo on the bread, and thin slices of cheese and tomato will do it. You've got the technique now, right? Okay, here are some other combinations: **Cheese and Pickle** (see page 88 for more on English pickle), **Chicken and Egg Salad** (with a little leaf lettuce), **Cream Cheese and Cucumber.**

To serve, stand the sandwiches on the flat end with the pointy end pointing up. If you mix sandwiches with different bread colors and ingredients on the same platter, you'll get a pretty effect and offer your family or guests a nice variety.

Variations: Well, this recipe has probably already offered a big enough variety, but try these menu ideas. These sandwiches go nicely with a simple soup like gazpacho or your favorite tomato soup, or they can be served at a birthday party or afternoon tea party.

The English Get in a Pickle

I have to say that what the English mean by "pickle" is a bit different than what I grew up on in South Texas. The English pickle is a jar of sweet-and-tangy, diced-and-pickled vegetables and fruits. I have found a brand called Branston Pickle Relish made by Crosse & Blackwell and imported by Nestlé USA that tastes quite authentic. Simply spread the pickle on one side of a slice of bread, put a smear of mayo and a slice of cheese on the other, trim crusts, slice on the diagonal, and set aside. If you're lucky, some of these will still be around by the time you get to eat!

Flaky Pizzas/Calzones

Skills taught/practiced: rolling out dough, baking.

Ingredients:
1 10-oz. can refrigerated flaky biscuits
Just enough flour to dust rolling pin and board
1/2 cup spaghetti sauce
1/2 cup chopped pepperoni (*or* Variations below)
1/2 cup shredded Parmesan *or* Romano cheese

Only if making calzones:
 1/4 cup melted butter
 1/2 tsp. dried oregano
 1/2 tsp. garlic powder

1. *Note*: An adult should turn on the oven and close-ly supervise its use. Preheat oven (conventional or toaster oven) to 400°F.

2. Split biscuits in half, and press or roll out each one to 2½-inch circle. (This is a perfect, non-critical time to practice using the rolling pin to make circles.)

Hint: One of my testers, Julianna, said a little flour on the cutting board and rolling pin was quite helpful.

If Making Pizzas:

1. Spoon about a teaspoon of sauce onto each bis-cuit half.

2. Sprinkle with a teaspoon of pepperoni or other topping of choice (see Variations below), and half a teaspoon of cheese.

3. Place on a lightly-greased cookie sheet (or a foil-lined toaster oven pan). Bake for 8 to 10 minutes, or until dough is lightly browned and cheese is bubbly.

If Making Calzones:

1. Melt the butter and mix in the oregano and garlic powder. Set aside, but keep warm.

2. Spoon about a teaspoon of sauce onto half (10) of the biscuit halves.

3. Sprinkle each with a teaspoon of pepperoni or other topping (see Variations below), and half a teaspoon of cheese.

4. Cover with a plain biscuit half and crimp edges with a fork.

5. Brush seasoned butter on the top of each calzone and place on a lightly-greased cookie sheet (or a foil-lined toaster oven pan).

6. Bake for 10 to 15 minutes, or until dough is lightly browned.

Makes 20 flaky pizzas or 10 flaky calzones.

Variations:
- *Use Canadian bacon, regular bacon, hamburger, Italian sausage, or chopped veggies, instead of pepperoni.*

Marble Eggs

Skills taught/practiced:
boiling, dyeing, handling hot foods safely.

Ingredients:
1 dozen eggs
1 kit of various-colored food-safe dyes
(using an Easter-egg kit is easiest)
Vinegar (if the egg-coloring kit calls for it)

1. Review safe stovetop usage (see pages 66-67). Put eggs in pot of water (enough to cover the eggs) on the stove and bring to boil. (You could drop them into boiling water, but that tends to crack the shell and let egg leak out into the water. It'll get cooked anyway, but it makes a mess.) Once the water is boiling, set the timer for 9-10 minutes.

2. Pour your dyes into disposable or color-safe containers. Find as many slotted spoons as you can. (If you don't have slotted spoons, regular ones will work but may be messier. Have paper toweling handy.)

3. When eggs are done, take out of water and let cool until they can be handled. (Sometimes I put the eggs in a bowl of water with ice cubes to help this process along.) Tap the egg all over hard enough *to crackle* the shell, but *do not break pieces off or peel the shell.*

4. Put the crackle-shelled eggs into the various dye baths and leave them as long as possible. I have refrig-

erated eggs overnight in dye baths; the long duration helped.

5. When you are ready to serve the eggs, peel them. The egg white should have taken on a marbled appearance.

These look really pretty laid out on a platter together, but try not to let them sweat and touch each other, or the color may run. The whole eggs also make a great edible centerpiece for a spring or Easter luncheon. You can lay them out in a basket on a bed of parsley or rosemary for an even nicer effect.

Variation:

- *If your platter is large enough, and if you are serving ham, surround the eggs with ham slices and garnish with a few leaves of parsley or rosemary.*

Easter Brunch

(good for any spring event)

For a festive Easter Brunch or other spring party, how about Marble Eggs (page 91) surrounded by a ring of ham slices cut about 1/4-inch thick? Serve with a Bibb 'n' Orange Salad (page 43) and Pink Soup (page 58). (If one of your eggs doesn't come out quite right, slice it and float the egg slices on top of the soup.)

Use pastel-colored table linens (paper is okay) and tableware.

For drinks, Mock Mimosas and Raspberry Cherry Fizz should do nicely. To serve Mock Mimosas, pour equal amounts of orange juice and club soda into a tall glass filled with crushed or cubed ice. For Raspberry Cherry Fizz, drop a couple of maraschino cherries into a tall glass filled with crushed or cubed ice (try to sandwich the cherries in the middle of the glass) and top with raspberry ginger ale.

Confetti Alphabetti

Skills taught/practiced:
cleaning produce, measuring, seasoning, presentation.

Ingredients:

1 16-oz. box dried alphabet pasta (see page 97)

2 tsp. salt

2 Tbsp. olive oil (note that more olive oil is called for below)

Pine nuts *or* walnuts; chop into small pieces after toasting

1 loosely-packed cup fresh Italian flat-leaf parsley

1/4 cup olive oil

1/4 cup lemon juice

1 red bell pepper

1 orange bell pepper *or* 1 parboiled carrot

1 yellow bell pepper *or* 1 cup corn kernels

1 zucchini

1 cup black olives

Salt

Pepper

1. Review safe cutting (pages 20-22) and cooktop (pages 66-67) procedures before beginning, and discuss use of the toaster oven if you are using it. Start the pasta water first and work on other parts of the recipe while you wait for it to come to a boil.

2. When your pasta water comes to a boil, pour in the whole box of alphabet pasta and two teaspoons of salt. Stir. Bring back to a boil and cook another 7-9 minutes. This small pasta shape is easy to over-cook, so start checking after about 6 minutes.

3. When the pasta is done, drain it into a colander, stir two tablespoons of olive oil into it, and set aside.

4. Toast the pine nuts (or walnut pieces) in a toaster oven or in a dry skillet on the stovetop until lightly browned. Set aside to cool. If using walnuts, chop into pea-sized pieces.

5. Rinse parsley and pat dry with paper towels. Remove stems and chop leaves coarsely. Mix in a large bowl (big enough to hold all ingredients) with 1/4 cup olive oil and 1/4 cup lemon juice, and set aside.

6. To prepare the peppers, remove the tops and seeds. (Save scraps in stock bag or compost bowl). Chop the peppers (and/or carrot) into pea-sized dice.

7. Clean the zucchini and chop the ends off. Cut 1/4-inch-thick slices off each side of the zucchini and keep the green skins on. (Save the core for another recipe or the stock bag.) Cut into pea-sized dice and add to bowl with parsley, olive oil, and lemon mixture.

8. If using canned black olives, rinse them in a colander and drain. If using olives stored in a jar with oil, simply remove olives from the jar and do not rinse. (In fact, if there is excess oil in the jar, you may want to use it in the salad for flavor.

Chop olives into—you guessed it—pea-sized dice and add to bowl.

9. Add cooked pasta and toasted nuts and toss all ingredients together thoroughly. Salt and pepper to taste.

You can serve this dish at room temperature or cold. Garnish with a few sprigs of parsley or other herb leaf if available.

Variations:

- *You can use a green bell pepper in place of the zucchini. I prefer the different texture and appearance of the zucchini, but the bell pepper adds more flavor.*
- *When you're selecting black olives, try to find some Kalamata for serious flavor! If you do, you may want to use some of the oil from the jar to enhance the flavor of your dish.*

Finding Alphabet Pasta

Some of you may remember this recipe from my gardening book, *A Guide to Happy Family Gardening*. Well, I love it a lot and I get so many compliments on it, I just wanted to include it for you here, too, with a little more detail on preparation. I call this recipe Confetti Alphabetti because it uses all the colors of the garden, as well as fun alphabet pasta. Kids love it!

If you don't regularly purchase dried alphabet pasta, look for Ronzoni brand Alphabets-51. If your grocer doesn't stock it, ask them to. It's manufactured by Hershey Pasta Group, Hershey, Pennsylvania, 17033-0815, or call 1-800-468-1714, or check Ronzoni's website: www.ronzoni.com.

Green Noodles

Skills taught/practiced: cleaning produce, measuring, seasoning, using food processor.

Ingredients:
  1/4 cup pine nuts *or* walnuts (perhaps more)
  2-4 cloves fresh garlic
  1/4 to 1/2 cup freshly grated or shredded
    Parmesan *or* Romano cheese
  2 cups tightly packed basil leaves
  1/4 cup olive oil (perhaps more)
  Salt and pepper
  1 lb. pasta (fresh or dried, flat or shaped)

1. Review safe cutting (pages 20-22) and stovetop procedures (pages 66-67) before beginning, and discuss use of the toaster oven, if you are using it. Toast the pine nuts (or walnut pieces) in a toaster oven or in a dry skillet on the stovetop until lightly browned. Set aside to cool. If using walnut pieces, chop to lima bean-sized pieces.

2. Chop the garlic into lima bean-sized pieces or smaller, and grate the cheese if it is not already grated.

3. Pack one cup basil leaves into a blender or food processor. Add half the (cooled) pine nuts, half the garlic, and half the cheese. Sprinkle in some salt, grind in some pepper, and drizzle with oil.

4. Top with remaining cup basil leaves and the other half of the pine nuts, garlic, and cheese. Sprinkle in

some salt, grind in some pepper, and drizzle with oil again.

5. Run the blender or processor, scraping down the sides as needed, until contents form a bright green paste. Add more olive oil if needed for the right consistency.

Note that all of these ingredient amounts are adjustable, so taste and see what you think. Spoon into containers (glass jars or plastic tubs) and top with a thin layer of olive oil to keep the pesto from oxidizing. It's okay if it does oxidize some at the top. That pesto is still perfectly edible; it's just not as pretty.

Pesto is traditionally served on a shaped pasta that will catch the sauce. (My son, Chandler, loves it on Wagon Wheels.) As you drain the pasta, save a little of the cooking water and use it to thin the sauce before stirring it into the pasta. That will help the sauce to coat the pasta evenly. But it's great on big, fat fettucini, too. Go with what you like!

Variations:

- Pesto is equally delicious with any other starch. Spread it on fresh or toasted bread (Bruschetta—see page 36); use it in or on a pizza crust.
- Toss it with steamed new potatoes and green beans for a special treat.
- Mix it into a risotto at the last minute before serving. Then sit back and collect the compliments!

Green Noodles and the Garlic Boy

Okay, this is really pasta with pesto sauce, but "green noodles" it became when Harper learned to talk, and Green Noodles it is in our house! Believe it or not, this is one of the most requested recipes around my kitchen, and not just because the Chief Cook likes it. If the kids get to choose the menu (in celebration of a birthday or good school performance, for instance), they pick this one pretty often.

And if you are concerned about the heavy garlic content . . . well, let me just tell you that kids can take a liking to the strangest things. One day when I was mincing garlic for a recipe, then-three-year-old Chandler ambled up and asked, "Whatcha doin', Mom?"

"Chopping garlic," says I.

"Can I have some?" Chandler asks, expectantly.

"No, garlic is too sharp and spicy to eat raw by itself," I reply, oh so reasonably.

Well, that "no" was a mistake. He dug in his heels, so I thought I would let the garlic teach him a lesson. Wrong again. He ate a clove's worth of minced garlic then and there. And yes, he still likes the flavor in foods, like our favorite pesto recipe, Green Noodles.

Quesadillas

Skills taught/practiced: cleaning produce, measuring, seasoning, presentation.

Ingredients:
1/2 lb. grated Colby Jack cheese
1/2 lb. cooked chicken
2 green onions
1 package flour tortillas (at least 10 tortillas)
Can of cooking spray
Bottled salsa of choice

1. Before beginning, review safe cutting (pages 20-22) and stovetop procedures (pages 66-67). Grate the cheese, if it is not already grated, and set aside.

2. Dice the chicken, if it is not already diced. Aim for pieces about the size of a lima bean. Set diced chicken aside (in a low-heat toaster oven for a while if you want warm ingredients).

3. Rinse green onions and peel off damaged or yucky outer leaves. Put in stock bag or compost bowl, or discard. Slice green onions into little 1/4-inch round pieces and set aside.

4. Set a flat-bottomed pan on the stove over low heat (a cast iron skillet is great: omelet and crepe pans usually work fine), or use an electric griddle, if you prefer.

If you've never put these together before, the process of making a Quesadilla is a lot like making a grilled cheese sandwich. You'll sandwich the fillings in a tortilla or between two tortillas, and simultaneously toast or grill the tortilla and melt the cheese inside around the other fillings.

For a Soft Quesadilla:

1. You don't need the cooking spray. Just warm two tortillas on either side briefly, then lay one tortilla down on the griddle, scatter a few pieces of chicken and green onion on it, top with cheese, and add the other warm tortilla.

2. Press down on the top tortilla with a spatula or egg turner to help the cheese adhere to all ingredients and to the inside of the tortilla.

3. After a minute or two, peek to see if the cheese is mostly melted and the bottom tortilla is warm if not brown (blackened is not good!).

4. If so, use the spatula to flip the tortillas over and grill the other side briefly, just until the cheese is good and melted and the tortilla lightly toasted. The tortillas should still be fairly soft.

5. Set aside on a plate lined with enough foil to wrap around the finished Quesadilla (a layer of paper towels inside the foil helps absorb condensation). Repeat as often as necessary until all tortillas or cheese is used up.

For a Crispy Quesadilla:

1. After warming the tortillas briefly, spray one side of one of the tortillas and lay it spray-side down on the

pan or griddle before beginning the filling-and-flipping process.

2. As the cheese is melting, just before you flip the Quesadilla, spray the top tortilla, and then flip it over to the down side.

3. Grill till lightly browned on both sides, and then set aside in foil as described in Step 5 above.

When all the Quesadillas are made, cut them into quarters and serve on a platter or individual plates. Serve with warmed salsa, cool Guacamole (page 23), or room-temperature Black Bean Dip (page 17).

Variations:

- If you have a market that sells Mexican cheeses, try some of their interesting melting cheeses. Ask your grocer for advice based on what's available.
- You can also use a mixture of cheddar and Monterey Jack cheeses, or—if your kids have a pretty good heat tolerance—try pepper jack.
- For alternate fillings, think in terms of peppers, mushrooms, other kinds of onions, bacon or sea-soned ground beef instead of chicken, or just cheese and veggies for a vegetarian alternative (my favorite!).
- Once, out of sheer desperation, I made them with frozen chicken nuggets; those were way too popular . . .

Desserts

Because many kids start cooking by making desserts, and because sweets are not hard to come by in 21st century America, I'm providing just a few dessert recipes. One is a healthy fruit salad made a bit more decadent with ice cream (or kept healthy with vanilla yogurt! You decide . . .). The others are very flexible recipes offering lots of variations that a child can work with over and over and become very competent preparing.

I Scream* Fruit Salad

Skills taught/practiced: cleaning produce, measuring, seasoning, presentation.

Ingredients:
   Use fruit you like, that is seasonal and
      plentiful in your area. Here are some
      ideas —
   1 cup fresh pineapple chunks
      or 1 10-oz. can pineapple chunks
   2 small oranges
      or 2 small cans mandarin oranges
   2 bananas
   10-12 fresh, pitted cherries *or* 1 small jar
      maraschino cherries
   3 kiwis
   2 small peaches
      or 1 10-oz. can sliced peaches
   1 large *or* 2 small apples
      (preferably Granny Smith, Fuji or Cameo)
   1 cup grapes, green or red or both
   1 cup pecans *or* walnuts *or* almonds *or*
      pine nuts (omit if your kids don't like nuts)
   1 quart vanilla ice cream *or* yogurt

1. If using canned fruits, an adult should open the cans. Help your child/ren drain the fruit, reserving the juice.

2. If using fresh fruits, wash and rinse each fruit (unless the skin will be peeled, as with oranges and bananas), and place on towels to dry. Leave skins on if they are edible, as with apples and grapes. Remove skins if they are inedible, as with kiwis.

3. Cut fruit into grape-sized chunks. (Grapes do not need to be cut, unless very small children will be eating some of the salad. Then everything needs to be cut very small, to about the size of half a grape.) Remove any pits or seeds and put fruit in bowl.

4. Chop nuts to pea-sized dice and pour into bowl.

5. Pour a little of the reserved juice over the salad, just enough to moisten all ingredients.

6. Cover salad bowl and refrigerate until ready to serve. The fruit will keep in good condition for about a day.

7. Serve in a bowl with ice cream or yogurt. You can either stir some ice cream or yogurt into the salad, or serve the salad in a bowl with the ice cream or yogurt alongside.

* If you're wondering about the title, that's a variant pronunciation of "ice cream."

Summer Bash

Even in north Texas, when it's summer, it's *hot*. And no matter how far north you live, you probably get some really hot days, too, which—Murphy's Law being what it is—will probably coincide with your big outdoor weekend plans! So, although hamburgers and fajitas and other grilled foods may be traditional for summer cookouts, I think the best approach for a summer bash is cooking *in* and then taking *out* for the picnic.

Foods served cool right out of a cooler are my favorite. They're very refreshing on a hot day, and they tend to be better for kids' cooking. These dishes go better than something that needs to be cooked over a hot grill in the heat of the day.

The best choices are recipes that tolerate refrigeration prior to serving and that can be served cool rather than hot or cold. The dips work well: Black Bean Dip (page 17) and Guacamole (page 23). The salads work well, too, especially the Greek Salad (page 49) and Bibb 'n' Orange (page 43). Confetti Alphabetti (page 94) makes a nice main dish, and a huge I Scream Fruit Salad (page 106) is a great dessert, especially if you are feasting at home, and can pull the ice cream out of the freezer right before serving.

Very Chocolate Cherry Cake

Skills taught/practiced:
measuring, mixing, baking, presentation.

Ingredients:
3 cups flour
2 cups sugar
1/2 cup baking cocoa
2 tsp. baking soda
1 tsp. salt
2 cups cold water
2/3 cup melted butter
     (*or* replace with peanut oil *or* applesauce)
4 tsp. vanilla extract
1 can cherries
confectioner's sugar

Note: This recipe works best in a bundt-type or a deep shaped pan (I use a heart-shaped pan). Review "Safe Oven, Safe Cook" section (pages 30-31) before beginning, and preheat the oven to 350°F. If you will be using a mixer, familiarize your child/ren with its safe operating rules.

1. An adult should open the canned cherries. Then a child can pour the cherries out into a colander with a bowl underneath to catch the liquid. Reserve this liquid.
2. Measure and mix dry ingredients in a large bowl

big enough to hold all ingredients: flour, sugar, cocoa, baking soda, and salt. Stir to combine.

3. In a large glass measuring cup, mix water, melted butter (or oil or applesauce), vanilla, and cherry juice from the can. Stir gently.

4. Pour into the dry ingredients, stirring until all ingredients are thoroughly combined. A few dry lumps are okay, but the batter should be pretty smooth.

5. Pour two-thirds of the batter into a well-greased cake pan, and then pour the cherries in. It's okay if they sink a little.

6. Then cover the cherries with the remaining batter.

7. Bake at 350°F for 30 minutes, or until top springs back. Turn out and let cool on a platter.

8. When you are ready to serve, sprinkle with confectioner's sugar. My kids like to spoon the sugar into a small strainer, and then knock it with a spoon to cause the sugar to sift out.

Variations:

- *You can use cherry pie filling, but be prepared to spoon the cherries out into the colander, or—if there's not much juice—straight onto the cake batter.*
- *If you don't like the sound of the cherry filling, or if you have some really ripe bananas that need to be used up, peel and smash up the bananas and mix them into the batter along with the wet ingredients; then you can omit the cherry filling.*

- *Or, you can use a different filling; whatever sounds good to you: blueberry pie filling? raspberry jam? orange marmalade? vanilla or banana pudding? A half-and-half mix of peanut butter and marshmallow crème? Let's see, that would be a Fluffer-Nutter Chocolate Cake! Yum . . .*

Apple Crumble

Skills taught/practiced:
cleaning produce, measuring, seasoning, presentation.

Ingredients:
6-8 cups sliced apples
   (preferably Granny Smith)
2 Tbsp. lemon juice
1/2 tsp. cinnamon
2/3 cup flour
1/2 cup brown sugar
1/2 cup rolled oats
1/3 cup butter
Vanilla ice cream (optional)

Note: Review the "Safe Cutting, Safe Cook" (pages 20-22) and "Safe Oven, Safe Cook" (pages 30-31) sections before beginning, then preheat the oven to 375°F.

1. Peel, slice, and core the apples (or substitute with blueberries, peaches, blackberries, or cranberries; if cranberries, add extra brown sugar to taste).
2. Put into a well-greased 2-quart baking dish.
3. Pour lemon juice over and sprinkle with cinnamon.
4. Mix the flour, brown sugar, and oats in another bowl and cut in butter until crumbly. (Little fingers can also mix the butter into the dry ingredients.)
5. Sprinkle this topping over the apples.

6. Bake at 375°F for 40 minutes. Serve warm out of the oven, with ice cream if you like.

 # Conclusion

Sounds easy enough, doesn't it? Go on . . . stir up a feast with your family's young cooks and together serve it up with a side of love!

Resources

MAGAZINES AND WEBSITES

Spider (ages 6 and up) and *Cricket* (ages 9 and up) magazines for children both feature a recipe in each issue tied to the theme of the issue (often cultural or holiday explorations). Recipes aside, these are great magazines. (See *Babybug*, too, by the same publisher. It's a magazine with cardboard pages to share with babies.) The subscription prices are rather high, but you don't see the ads for video games or violent toys that clutter up the pages of many other magazines. Call 1-800-827-0227 for subscription information. *Spider* and *Cricket* are published by Carus Publishing Co., 315 Fifth Street, Peru, IL, 61354.

Crayola Kids: Family Time Fun is a magazine full of crafts and projects for parents and kids to do together, and each issue includes recipes designed for parent and kids working together. For subscription information, call 1-800-846-7968, or write to them at Meredith Corporation, 1716 Locust Street, Des Moines, IA, 50309-3023.

This magazine has a sister website at **www.crayolakids.com** with activity ideas, including seasonal recipes, and lots of other fun stuff to do.

Family Fun Magazine is a magazine for parents, but includes lots of crafts and things to do with kids. The magazine includes a section for parental cooking ideas in every issue, as well as a department called "Cooking Class: A Step by Step Guide to Teaching Kids to Cook." Some of these recipes emphasize cuteness over kid do-ability, but you can't sneeze at the idea of your kids learning 12 new recipes a year. For subscription information, call 1-800-289-4849, or write to Family Fun, PO Box 37032, Boone, IA, 50037-0032 (*note*: this is the subscription service, not the editorial offices).

RESOURCES

This magazine also has a sister web site at **www.family-fun.com**, where you can find more recipes and craft ideas, as well as areas describing party ideas and upcoming events.

In addition, my browser of choice (**www.google.com**) brings up over 3,000 links when I search on "cooking with kids." Yours will probably bring up more than a few, too. Here are some that I liked.

The Kids Cooking Corner site at **www.kidscookingcorner.com** is a by-kids, for-kids effort put together by Hillary and her sister Ali (and perhaps their Mom, one supposes). It only listed one recipe when I visited, but scroll down to the Archive link and you'll find lots more.

The **Love @ Home** website at **www.loveathome.-com** is "an internet resource for above average families (those with more than 2.2 kids)." In addition to forums on all sorts of topics, recipes can be found at **www.loveathome.com/dinner.htm**.

Weekly Reader's website features "Cooking fun for parents and kids in grades Pre-K, K, and 1." For recipes, check out **www.weeklyreader.com/features/cookwka.html**.

The National Pork Board has a **Cooking With Kids** website that you may be wondering why I am telling you about (is she a pork farmer in her spare time? Um, no . . . but I do like the occasional bit of ham!). Well, this site provides a surprising amount of useful information on tools and cooking techniques that'll teach any parent a thing or two. Point your browser to **www.nppc.org/ForKids/cookingkids.html**. Many of the tips are provided by an expert from the "Kids in the Kitchen" network of the International Association of Culinary Professionals.

Cook's Prayer

Lord, bless their little hands
　that are learning to help
　and learning to make
　so that hungry people might be fed
　not just for a day, but for a lifetime

And Lord, bless my big hands
　help me to be patient, when I already know how
　and to be tender, when what we make is a mess
　and to be kind, so that those pairs of little hands
　will always be willing, now and forever

And Lord, bless the food we make
　for we know it came from your hands first
　and your blessing passes through us to the
　　people we feed
　may it ever be so, in my kitchen and my
　　children's kitchen.

Amen

Index

118

A GUIDE TO HAPPY FAMILY COOKING

A GUIDE TO HAPPY FAMILY COOKING

About the Author

Tammerie Spires has been messing around in the kitchen since childhood and enjoys cooking with her kids, Harper (6) and Chandler (4), and husband, David.

As evidenced by the food tips in *A Guide to Happy Family Camping* (Good Books), and the recipes in *A Guide to Happy Family Gardening* (Good Books), Tammerie believes good food is integral to good fun.

Now, in her third book, *A Guide to Happy Family Cooking,* Tammerie provides lots of Recipe and Resource information about foods to mix, make, bake, store, freeze, give . . . and *enjoy* to help your family's children and adults cook together happily.

Tammerie is a native Texan, nine-year resident of Richardson, recent escapee from a 15-year career in corporate communications, and happy to be spending time writing, doing volunteer work (Peace Mennonite Church, Dallas North Montessori School), and hanging out with her husband and kids, preferably around a bowl of Green Noodles!

She is also a student at Brite Divinity School and Eastern Mennonite Seminary.